OH NO!

"NOW MY KNOT IS COMING APART!"

TOP ISSUES THAT THREATEN HAPPY MARRIAGES

BY

CARLETON & ANGELA BOOKER

DEDICATION

To our daugther Erika we miss you so much! Not a day go by that we don't think about you, WE LOVE YOU. To be **absent from the body is to be present with the Lord** (2 Cor. 5:8).

Date of home going September 15, 2006

Love

Mom and Dad.

Forward

This book is a practical tool that will help you discover the power of forgiveness, trust, healing and complete restoration in your marriage. Carleton and Angela Booker have walked an incredible journey in their marriage and through Jesus they have forged forward and experienced firsthand the power of restoration. Carleton and Angela have keen insight into how God's people encounter God's power and then give expression to it in their lives and walk in it together in the covenant of marriage. They are a couple after God's own heart and they speak from their experience of God's heart and His power to heal and restore. This book will encourage and challenge you with insight and the necessary tools to pursue and experience marriage God's way. It will set you on a course of seeing the fulfillment of a happy and loving marriage become a reality. I pray as you read this book you will be inspired to partner with God and with each other and dream big in God. You are called to shine for Jesus and your marriage is destined to win! Bert & Kim Moreno, Senior Lead Pastors *The Worship Center, Antioch California*

What couples are saying about the Booker's

We bless the almighty for leading us through this marriage journey, and giving us the grace to and share and enjoy the experience.

Trust, Forgiveness and Healing,

We have known Pastor Carleton and Angela Booker for about 35 years. Their love, friendship, and strength have stood the times of hardship, lost, test and trials in their lives and in their marriage. We have seen them stand and trust the Lord to be God in their lives, to comfort them, to heal them, to restore them, to replenish them, to establish them and to uphold them with His Right Hand.

We have seen them, when their marriage stood the test of trust. We have seen them stand, believe and trust God when their precious daughter Erika passed away from cancer and they had to endure the pain, and the grief, of her passing. When their very successful business suffered, and when Angela was diagnosed with cancer.

Through it all they held on to the hand of Jesus Christ, to take them through these difficult times in their lives. They put their trust in the Lord to sustain them, to up hold them and to strengthen them. We have seen the manifestation and demonstration of Jesus Christ working in their lives and in their marriage.

To God Be the Glory,

With Great Love,

Pastor's Arthur & Eva Thomas

Pastor's Carleton & Angela Booker married us on July 12, 2010 and continue to this day to be very good friends and mentors. Over the years they have guided us out of many storms, often even coming to our home in the middle of the night to talk and pray us through a heated battle.

One of the things that I absolutely love about them is their transparency. Their lives and marriage ministry teach and sometimes even show us that we are human and bound to have many trials, but none too big for God if we allow Him to always be present. Their example of marriage places a heavy emphasis on forgiveness and how it must be freely and frequently extended. Through their teachings and examples, we have learned how to be courageous and patient in difficult times, respect each one's boundaries, but most importantly to just love one another unconditionally. I think we both would agree that without the guidance of team Booker and their Godly influence in our lives we wouldn't be married today. We love them dearly and are very thankful for their friendship and ministry.

Jose & Melissa Mixon

My wife and I have been married for almost two years now. We are very happy and hold the tools and skills to maintain a Holy and prosperous marriage, thanks to God using Pastor Carleton and Angela Booker's Special Forces Marriage Class. We were unsaved and engaged for about 8 years prior. We got saved and continued to keep the status of being engaged until we were invited to these marriage classes being taught by Pastor Carleton and Angela Booker. I was amazed at the insight that we learned in just the first three classes we attended. Pastor Carleton and Angela are the real deal. They have been married for a long time and have been through the good and the bad and have always kept Jesus in the forefront of their relationship keeping it alive and Holy. I would recommend this class for all engaged or married couples of all ages. The Highest God has put an anointing on these two that you are going to want a double portion of!!! This was not just a marriage counseling class, this class gave us the tools we needed to have a healthy, Holy and yes happy relationship. Thank you, Pastor Carleton and Angela, for your heart in serving God and helping Krystal and I get on track.

Sincerely

Gabriel and Krystal Aguilar

We met Pastor Carleton and Angela Booker in 2009 while attending another church. At the time we were growing in the Lord and our marriage had improved a lot. We heard there was a marriage ministry class on Sundays before service and we wanted to try it but never made the time. One day as we walked thru the campus, Pastor Carleton was passing. He greeted us with the warm smile and asked us if we wanted to go to the marriage class called

Families on Fire. We thanked him politely and we said, "No thank you, our marriage is good". Immediately he replied "well if your marriage is good then come and teach the class next week." Right away my husband responded; "well, it's not that good!" Sure, enough we were there next Sunday- not to teach but to learn. From that day forward we wouldn't miss a Sunday of Families on Fire. We learned so much from Pastor's Carleton and Angela we asked them to become our personal marriage mentors. The Lord gave us a heart for marriage. We now lead the marriage ministry at our current church and every time we mentor couples we mention Pastor Carleton & Angela and how they impacted our marriage.

Rene & Maria Aguirre

We have had the good fortune of knowing Carlton Booker and his wife, Angela, since 2013. During the time we have known them we have been astonished watching them walking out their wedding vows of for better or for worst, in sickness and in health. This has been a blessing to us. It has helped strengthen our marriage to see marriage and not just idealistically. We have had many opportunities to attend their in-home "First-Friday" marriage get-togethers. The "First-Friday" is an event in which married, engaged, and dating couples meet in the Booker's home to build marital relations by use of various teaching methods such as videos and group discussions. The meetings take place the first Friday evening of every month. Their formal marriage conference was also phenomenal. This couple has been realistic, honest, and transparent in their teachings proving their desire to elevate other marriages while giving God all the glory! "As iron sharpens iron, so one person sharpens another" Proverbs 27:17 (NIV).

John and Sharon Smalls

Marriage Ministry Leaders

Carleton, you and Angela are simply amazing. Your passion for each other has inspired your ability to speak truth about issues in marriage and bring healing to so many couples. It has been our pleasure, honor, and privilege to be one of those many couples. Changing the world one marriage at a time. Passion isn't something that you learn. It is a natural born desire to strive, to be better every day than you were the day before. Passion describes you and Angela to a tee. Your desire to help and assist other couples to love one another, but to strive and desire to make their marriage better is simply beyond explanation. You two are AMAZING!!

Kevin & Michell Kern

Being loving friends for over 20 years you get to see the challenges and achievements along the journey of life and in the ups and downs you find out who your true friends are we were there in the depths of our life in the highs of our life together a family, staying strong together no matter what was happening. I can always call you and you can always call me, and we walk through this journey of life as family members since the mid to late 90s and we are still walking on this journey together as a family. Helen and I, and Jeff Jr. love you guys and there is no greater love than friendship that is always there no matter what. From business to personal you both always have been leaders in the church and around the community. You have raised two beautiful children who have those same attributes. I still tear up when I looked into your eyes as I was remembering the season you both went through when your daughter passed away. I've never cried at funerals before, but I cried at your daughters. Because of the loss of your daughter and because of the pain I saw a father and mother go through, losing their oldest child. As an owner of a mortuary, I deal with the passing of people every day and I owned the mortuary that buried your daughter. So, I say all that just to say this, I've never met a more phenomenal couple who was able to deal with whatever life brought them with a smile in the courage that God had placed in their lives. It has always been my privilege to be your friend, your brother for life!

Mr. Jeffrey Lee Lynn Butler Sr.

Table of Contents

From the Author's

What a Road trip! My wife and I are celebrating over 40 years of marriage, and we are grateful to the King of Kings for keeping us along the journey of marriage. We just want to share a few words of inspiration and encouragement in this book. With all up and coming young and vibrant couples, to empower them on this journey along the path of marriage.

If it wasn't for the Lord on our side, leading us on; we would have given up on this road trip a longtime ago. Together, and with the help of God, we have come to learn that life is a road trip and so is marriage. To embark on this road trip of marriage it will require significant levels of faith, trust and hope. It will demand patience, longsuffering, forgiveness, and understanding of the each other on this road trip.

Most often, we give up, not because of the road trip. But the character, attitude, and behavior of our partners, which sometimes diverts the focus, attention, and direction of going on the road trip.

Just as there are many traffic lights on the streets or roads we drive on, there are also traffic lights of marriage that try to stop us on the road trip of marriage. These traffic lights on the roads do not stop us permanently. They just slow us down for a little while and then vroom! We zoom off toward our destination.

Now, marriage traffic lights are not there to stop us from the vision, purpose, and direction of the union we have entered, but to slow us down when we are speeding off into a dangerous road ahead. It is our behaviors and responses that stop the road trip of marriage.

There are challenges in every marriage, and it takes the grace of God, prayer, the word, purpose for couples to stay on the route of marriage. There is nothing like a marriage made in heaven. Marriages are created God and meant to be enjoyed. This means a married couple must learn to have a focus, direction, vision, and purpose for their journey here on earth.

There are many things couples can to do to maintain a safe journey on the highway for this road trip. And in this book, we would like to highlight the need for effective communication in marriages, as one of the ways to enjoy the road trip of marriage. Effective communication kept us for these 40 years, and we are still journeying along gracefully.

It takes two people to have a productive conversation at any level. This implies that for people or couples to have a stable relationship, they must ensure that communications are established in the heart of their relationship to start with. Two people cannot walk together except they agree and the only thing that makes that possible is effective communication.

Couples should be able to feel free to talk about "anything" without their partner feeling undermined, disregarded or disrespected. One of the main reasons that relationships don't efficiently work is because people are not talking or refusing to communicate as they should, thus causing each other pain and frustration within the relationship.

It is true that people are different, based on their backgrounds, values, outlooks or views (perceptions) which create different comfort zones for them. Talking about issues or challenges within the relationship is seen as a hurdle. This discourages them from talking about serious issues within their relationship because they do not want to be seen by their partners as nagging or causing trouble.

When people do not talk about issues within their relationships, it creates unnecessary misunderstanding, distance, indifference, competition, aggression and often verbal violence toward each other because issues have not been discussed.

Relationship is the center of our lives, and it takes communication to express the love we have for each other. When this is achieved, it can easily lead to feelings of joy, lightheartedness, inner peace, contentment with life, and a deep inner wisdom with each other.

Therefore, this book is written to help rebuild relationships that are on the verge of break-up. It serves as a fence-builder to prevent other relationships from driving into the ditch of separation especially when the partners pay attention to effective communication.

Although it is a fact that some people find it difficult to talk about their personal experiences like childhood relationships that ended up badly, or their past life, due to past hurt. Often talking about those experiences will create a transparent relationship.

Openness in marriage increases the love and affection partners feel for each other. As partners embrace their differences, they learn to communicate more efficiently, openly, and without fear of judgment, and with respect. They would be able to avoid unnecessary misunderstandings that has plagued many relationships, causing hurt, anger, confusion and often painful divorces.

We hope that you learn a thing or two from this book. Marriage has been a beautiful experience for us, and we have been privileged to learn from our journey. We hope that through sharing our experiences we can help you find strength to work toward a more fulfilling marriage.

Pastor's Carleton & Angela.

PREFACE

We believe no person gets married with the intention of getting divorced. But these things happen. And that's why marriage coaches can be helpful. A marriage coach helps people resolve marital issues that they might not be able to resolve on their own. Many couples have tried marriage counseling but have not benefited from that approach. Partnering with a marriage coach can offer more extensive tools.

We are marriage coaches, and the technique we use takes a different approach toward tackling marital issues that may ordinarily lead to the dissolution of marriages. There are certain cases where counseling suffices to provide help, but coaching creates action, and action brings change. Coaching does not just solve the immediate marital challenge, it also teaches coules fundamental ideals that are necessary for building a strong marital foundation and achieving a stronger, more lasting structure.

If you feel that for some reason, your marriage is stuck. We can help you move past that blockage, as we bring 41 years' experience to aid you on your journey. Before you consider throwing in the towel, ask yourself this question, 'what will happen in five years, if things don't change?' If you are not comfortable answering that question, maybe it is time to seek help.

We offer you the support you need to make your marriage work. All you need to do is follow at **www.coachmarriagecouplesbyacouple.com** and make an appointment for a strategic plan for change in your marriage. We lay out a 12-session course at your disposal. These sessions will expose you to concepts and valuable tools to effectively change your marriage into a satisfying one. With the right tools your marriage will thrive.

In today's world, our culture doesn't value the interdependence of a healthy team. The culture values independence and puts it above everything else it's all about a 'me' mentality. To have a loving partnership there needs to be a level of inter-dependence involved, which will make your bond stronger.

Marriage is challenging, it is serious work. Both couples often bring a truckload of past hurts and baggage into the relationship. That's we move in extreme transparency. We keep it "100".

No kumbaya, no rainbows, and stars. We reveal more about ourselves and our marriage and the challenges we've had to overcome in our forty plus years together. You may want to put your seat belt on at this time!

It is our hope that through our openness and experiences, you may pick up a thing or two and, in the end learn how to communicate in love. Love is non-negotiable, love is learning how to forgive, and trust again. Love is overcoming the loss of a child, moving past the loss of a family business, taking all those hurts, pain, and circumstances that seek to drive a wedge between you and your partner, and instead allowing those seasons in your lives to bring strength and determination to succeed no matter what life throws your way. You can live your marriage vows. It doesn't matter whether you are just starting out on the marriage journey, or you are working hard to get your relationship on track, or attempting to save your marriage, this book is for you. We are on a mission to stomp out divorce in the world. We desire to see people triumph through marital challenges. That's our priority.

Are you ready to get off on your journey to marital fulfillment? If you are sure you are ready, then do these things:

TAKE THE FIRST STEP

One quick and easy way to start repairing your rocky relationship is to take the free couple's questionnaire on Coaching Married Couples by a Couple. Empowering married couples to love forever. The website:

www.coachmarriagecouplesbyacouple.com

STEP OUT TWO BY TWO

A happy marriage relationship is a synchronized relationship. We work better as part of a team. Any team requires coordination and working together. Just like in a 3-legged race, if you don't coordinate with your team member, you'll trip, fall, and get hurt by trying to go your own way. Step out as two merged into one. The decision to work toward a happier marriage is a joint decision between partners. Before you start out, ensure that your partner is committed and willing to walk with you.

HERE'S THE SOLUTION.

We have found that a lack of safe emotional connections an unwillingness to forgive and change is the cause of many relationship struggles.

Our approach is to help couples rediscover the safe connection they felt when they first fell in love. Once this connection is re-established, and the couples truss each other again, and work out their future problems without third party intervention, then our work is done. We are passionate about this mission to end divorce in the world. We believe that this book will reveal to you the challenges that threaten happiness in marriages. And give you tools to succeed!

CHAPTER ONE

THE KNOT

And if one prevails against him, two shall withstand him; and a three-strand cord is not quickly broken. Ecclesiastes 4:12

Oh, I am so excited! We are going to tie the knot on Saturday! Well I'm sure you've heard that statement ... **what is the meaning of the phrase 'Tie the knot'?**

Pretty dumb question, right? But let's just get it out of the way. The expression "to tie the knot" means "to get married." This is not a new concept in human history. In several cultures around the world, tying a knot serves as a symbol of enduring, everlasting and eternal love. The knot signifies a bond between the lovers, it has always been a symbol of unity and togetherness of the parties involved.

Tied knots as a symbol of love and marriage were especially popular in the Roman culture. Young brides often wore a belt or girdle tied in a Hercules Knot at their wedding. Only the groom was allowed to untie it (the untying of which was supposed to be a further symbol of childbearing). This knot was supposed to represent the binding character of the marriage oath.

A Hercules Knot:

Knot tying as a symbol of marital bond did not only exist in the Roman culture, there also exist the *true-Love's Knot* from Scotland, England, and Denmark. This knot stands as a symbol of love and fidelity to one's beloved. It is for this reason that ribbons with true-love knots were often given out as bridal favors at weddings. In Great Britain, they put these ribbons in their hats. In France, they were worn around the arm. At first, the ribbons came in different colors, but eventually, just white ones were used.

A True-love's Knot.

In Hindi wedding ceremonies, they tie together the bride's garment to the groom's scarf. This is supposed to symbolize a life-long bond. The knot is not to be untied until the marriage ceremony has been completed.

Translating all these ceremonial rites and significance into the realm of marriage, one may ask, what does it all mean? It would not be unsafe to say that marriage as ordained from the onset is a knot. Marriage ought to be an inseparable bond, holding two people together. Why is this? Well, it takes two ends to make a knot. These two ends come from different backgrounds, these two people have had different experiences and family just like the materials that may be used to tie the knots could be from different origin and have different histories.

The marital knot we refer to, is the knot that holds partners *until death do them part*. In other words, ideally, only death is the escape from marriage. Today however, there may be other reasons why this knot maybe untied, but those reasons must be such that makes a lot of sense. Some of the reasons that would be sensible enough to lead to divorce or separation may include abuse, or maltreatment. Any other excuse, including cheating is not a good enough reason.

To this end, we must first warn that tying the knot is a thing for adults. When we talk about adults, we refer to people who are willing to have an open mind with regards to the partnership that they are about to enter. We refer to people who are willing to make things work, taking each other into consideration, praying for each other and supporting each other all the way through. We cannot stress this, marriage is a life time commitment. You must choose your partner wisely, prepare for it and do all you can, to make it work. Tying the knot is serious business for serious minded people only.

Tying the knot commits you to that one person who alone you are to share the rest of your life with. Marriage is all about commitment, hard work, conceding to the will of the other person, sharing, and generally being in a partnership.

We have said that this knot binds the partners into an eternal partnership in which they have both made an agreement, together as partners to love, trust and respect each other. Even though partners make this vow of commitment almost every week, very few keep to their vows. Before long, a lot of couples will often file for divorce, dragging their children through horrible experiences.

In the next few chapters, we will consider some of these things that often lead to challenges that threaten even good marriages. Keep reading, and don't forget to look out for those points that you might relate to, those points that you can identify with as the problems plaguing your marriage.

CHAPTER TWO

IN OR OUT OF BOUNDS

Out-of-bounds in sports is being beyond or passing the limits or boundaries of a field, course, etc., marking the area within which the ball or puck is legally in play. Beyond any established boundaries or prescribed limits; prohibited; forbidden.

Marriage is one amazing, yet confusing pact. One minute they tell you that marriage comprises of the man and woman alone in a union of soul that serves to convert two separate individuals into one whole. The next minute, they tell you to watch out for boundaries.

The truth is yes, marriage is a union. Yes, the two people are still humans, despite this union. They are two humans, learning to live as one, two humans, learning to take each other into consideration, learning to share life lessons and the experiences they are faced with daily. Despite the union, they both still have their individual differences likes and dislikes and it is only when the partners deliberately seek for ways to merge these differences and turn them into a beautiful harmony that a healthy marriage is born.

Despite having established a good foundation for your marriage, things could still go south for a lot of reasons. There can never be a healthy relationship if the parties do not know where to stop and go. What is life without direction? When partners do not know what constitutes the boarders, it could be a problem.

As we mentioned earlier, we all have our likes and dislikes. We all have what we want, and what we cannot tolerate. Understanding this requires us to take into cognizance those things the other person likes and dislikes to allow for the continuous flow of the oil of marital bliss.

Only when a husband and wife know and respect each other's needs, choices, and freedom can they give themselves freely and lovingly to one another. Boundaries are the "property lines" that define and protect husbands and wives as individuals. Once these boundaries are in place, a good marriage can become better, and a less than satisfying one can even be saved.

When two people are in love, there might not be boundaries. But when love translates into marriage, there is a need to draw limits. Setting rules and guidelines ensure that both the partners are happy and know where they need to stop. That helps keep the marriage healthy for a lifetime.

For a relationship to be successful and healthy, you need to be happy with yourself before attempting to make your spouse happy. Boundaries help you achieve that and more; they make you take responsibility for your actions instead of blaming it on your spouse. With boundaries in place, both people will have greater understanding in knowing their responsibilities. This helps iron things out.

Setting boundaries helps resolve conflicts and will help to prevent you and your partner from being hurt. It gives you the power to change things for good as you are in control of your actions. And further aids to strike a balance between you and your spouse's priorities.

All couples go through conflicts in their lives. Some lack intimacy despite having no real problems, while others make sacrifices and yet are not happy in the relationship. Some partners don't take responsibility, and even cheat on their spouse. The problems may be different, but the confusion, pain, and ambiguity are the same. Boundaries prevent such problems and play a vital role in a marriage.

Setting boundaries means learning to say *NO*, and learning when to say *NO*. We all need our space at one time or the other. That is what makes life bearable. But it will be wise to remember always that when we set boundaries, we also need to know when to compromise. When those boundaries are pushing away your spouse, then, it is time to review them and make adjustments.

Bear in mind, *the marriage is not about you alone*. If you like to spend one or two hours alone, undisturbed just as a way of cooling off after a stressful day, it is not a bad idea, once your spouse understands that this is the way you like to relax. But once it starts to take away from the joy you ought to derive from your marriage, then find a way around it.

It is not only your spouse that needs to respect boundaries, there are also other people who were in your life prior to your marriage who maybe had certain privileges in your life. Those people would need to come into the new reality of your marriage. You must learn to set limits for the outsiders. Once you are married, the two are considered to be one. It means that no third party should see or say anything.

Let your mother know that there is a limit to her contributions to your life. Let your father know that you now have someone else, and that together with that person you have decided to make a life with them. Your friends are now friends to the both of you, jointly. They are not entitled to take sides or gossip about your relationship. Their advice is not necessary since it would be most likely biased, being that often they only have your version of the story. Therefore you need a marriage coach. Coaches see and hear both sides.

Your parents and friends are not coaches, they are not skilled at helping you work out your marital challenges, at best, they can only give you some suggestions, gleaned from their own experiences. And those suggestions may not work for you and your spouse. Kick out unnecessary third-party distractions and focus on making your marriage work.

We have established that it is necessary to define limits and set boundaries, but how do we go about that without causing too many problems? One of the ways to set boundaries is to start out respecting boundaries. Before you announce to your partner certain limits, set an example by coming up with boundaries for yourself also. Identify those areas your spouse has complained about and begin to consciously make the necessary changes.

We all know what hurts our spouse. It maybe something as trivial as not doing the dishes, leaving the toothpaste a certain way, leaving the house untidy, or touching their personal things. Whatever it is, try to avoid doing that and respect your partner's boundaries. Learn to give the other person breathing space, no matter whether you are single or married. We always seek for that one thing we can call our personal thing. It doesn't matter whether you are married, that personal tendency still lingers in the background, as a result, you must learn to respect those idiosyncrasies and differences that makes your partner a distinct human being.

CHAPTER THREE

TALKING VS. COMMUNICATION

" The first goal of conversation is achieving understanding, not necessarily reaching an agreement".

At the core of every healthy marriage is the ability of a couple to communicate with each other successfully. Communication can be tricky because individuals have different backgrounds, experiences, and sometimes even culture. All these affect communications. Also, 60 to 90% of all communication consists of body language, eye contact, facial expressions, and tone rather than words. As a result, communication goes beyond words. How you say it, the feeling you have conceived before you say it, the thought behind the words and the circumstances surrounding the statement will be taken into consideration when your partner is interpreting your words.

Communication is a skill that must be learned and practiced to have a successful marriage. It has a great deal to do with interpretation and it is a core aspect of marriage that fosters understanding. If couples do not communicate, they cannot understand each other. Imagine yourself in a country where you do not know how to speak the same language as they do. It would be challenge even with an interpreter, it may still not be easy to reach an understanding. But if you are acquainted with the language, you can better relate with the people. That is what communication is all about, it is all about speaking the same or similar language with your spouse and coming to a point of understanding.

No relationship is perfect and problem-free all the time. From our experience, we have come to learn that marriage takes work, commitment, communication and reevaluating the way you communicate. What are your expectations, and what you both need to work on? Marriage means questioning yourself, checking to make room for the other person all the time and just generally taking each other into consideration.

But it is not necessarily hard, and it shouldn't be. Yes, there are some issues in a marriage that seem to be more common than others, while some are just peculiar. But when you take a good look at the root cause of these things, these problems most likely exists because of lack of connection. Connection is the key to a good marriage, and the stronger the communication is, the more connection there will be. To put it another way – excellent communication in a marriage resolution in a strong connection.

We feel connected to God the most, when we pray and learn from the word. Prayer is a way of bringing our thoughts and lay it open to the master. When your prayer life is active, your connection to God is stronger. This would then mean that you will be more open to receiving inspiration from God. Your connection to God thus derives from your communication in prayer. When you feel the most connected to God, check your prayer life. But when you don't feel connected to God, it may be that your prayer life is dwindling.

Here is another illustration that points out the need for communication as an essential ingredient in strengthening connection. When you go out with your friend, you find out that the friend you speak to the most are those you have come to connect with. How did you come to connect with these people? At one point or the other, you began talking and realized that *hey! I like this person.* They presented a bit of themselves to you, and you laid out a bit of yourself to them, and things just clicked.

Again, what happened to those friends you made some time ago when you were in college, or before you moved to another city. Why did you suddenly grow apart? You were all chummy friends then, what happened? You stopped hanging out together, you stopped talking to each other every day and slowly, you drifted apart. In other words, you lost connection with that person, because you stopped communicating.

Communication is the first step to developing a connection. You cannot know someone you have not met or talked to. Even though communication is essential to building a connection, communication in words is not all that is necessary when you have attained that connection. This is the heightened point of communication, but for now, we are interested in the basics. So, it will suffice if we know those little things that help couples move beyond talking and into the realm of real communication.

Here are a few tips on how to improve communication in your marriage:

1. LISTEN

There is a reason why it is called communication. It is a two-way thing and it is not only about you. While you also need to be heard, you need to allow others speak. And you must be genuinely willing to listen to what that person has to say. This listening goes beyond hearing the words alone, it also has to do with sifting out the feelings of the speaker and relating to those feelings in relation to the spoken words.

"The best type of communication involves mutual respect, validation of feelings, active listening and a willingness to compromise and negotiate" Only marriages where couples provide support for each other around personal concerns such as work and friendship last.

2. COMMUNICATE WITHOUT PRESSURE

When both spouses are working, and financial pressures have intensified, couples find it difficult to find time to talk there issues out. Find time to talk and express all those feelings gathered from work and other engagements. It is better to take time resolve issues calmly, talking through things than trying to explain the reasons for your actions when you're under severe pressure or in the heat of an argument. Straightening out issues during arguments is rarely an effective means of addressing problems.

Couples should always make time to talk and express their feelings. During this time of expression, partners are most likely to reach a solution to the problems bothering them. Once this pressure is out of the way, the communication process becomes easier. Just sharing your thoughts and feelings with those you love relieves you from a lot of stress and you can move on developing a better relationship.

3. SHOW CARE AND CONCERN

What's critical in sustaining positive communication is being understood and cared for. We all want to be loved, we all want to feel that someone else is involved and feels what we feel, that someone else understands. Who else is in a better position to feel as you feel other than your spouse? When your spouse does not show that they care or understand, it becomes a problem in marriage.

Partners need a reaffirmation that the other person understand what they feel. For example, a couple has agreed to go on a special date together while the kids are staying with their grandparents, but a spouse must cancel due to a work emergency at the last minute. Ordinarily, this could lead to a disagreement that could appear like you are more concerned about your work more than you are about your spouse. At this point, it would be easier if the offending spouse gave a reply that explains the situation and shows genuine concern, care and interest in the things that may have disappointed or hurt the other person. So, it would be wise to say in reply, "I know how important this weekend was to you. I have no choice but to work this weekend. We will reschedule, and I will make it up to you." That sounds a lot better that "I have got to work, it is not my fault that I have to work". Communicating with empathy and caring for each other strengthens the relationship

4. AVOID LEAVING YOUR PARTNER IN THE SHADOWS

We have seen many marriages dissolve. When one spouse feels "invisible," this often leads to a breach in communication, and it is one of the leading causes of divorce. When you make your spouse feel invisible, you make them feel like their opinion is not needed, or that they do not matter. Once a partner starts feeling denied, not listened to and overlooked, that marriage is likely headed for doom.

You need to make your spouse a priority and to achieve this communication is of utmost importance. When you don't display your spouse as an important part of your life, you make him or her feel invisible.

5. FIGHTS ARE INEVITABLE

Conflict in marriage is normal, every couple has their own problems. What makes most marriages enviable however, is the ability of both parties to put their heads together and seek a way to move their marriage forward after a conflict.

Couples that survive hard times show an ability to repair the relationship, Disagreements are going to happen, but couples who can talk things out, listen to one another, and make repairing the problem a priority without abuse.

Let every quarrel and argument be adequately addressed to result in an effective change. Don't quarrel or fight for the love of it. When you have an argument, take time out, to fix the problem once you both cool off.

6. WHEN IN DOUBT, SEEK HELP

If your car doesn't start, you take it to a mechanic. If your teeth are in pain, you call the dentist. But when a marriage turns sour, many people keep digging, and sinking deeper, and they remain reluctant to seek help. Marital coaching can help unravel a couple's problems and get them to refrain and adjust how to communicate.

7. AVOID THE "DUMPING EVERYTHING ON YOUR PARTNER" SYNDROME

Throwing the "kitchen sink" at one partner involves bringing up every injustice, infraction and slight the partner has inflicted on the other partner last year, two years ago and on the first date. That is a no-no. Instead of raising every past indiscretion, focus on specific and recent behavior that trouble you and look for the solutions together. Forget whatever injustices that happened a decade ago and all such actions and inactions that ought to be long forgotten.

8. LEARN TO AVOID PUSHING THE BUTTONS

Most couples inevitably push each other's buttons. When the wife criticizes her husband housekeeping, it reminds him of his mother's criticism. When the husband raises his voice and begins to get agitated, the wife is reminded of her father's anger and gets bent out of shape. We recommend that couples must be conscious of what each other's buttons are and try to avoid them.

If the wife is upset by her husband's getting angry, the husband should consciously speak in a slow, measured tone so she can listen. If the husband is reminded of his critical mom, the wife should withhold some of her criticism of her husband housekeeping and choose her battles wisely.

CHAPTER FOUR

TIME MANAGEMENT

Why is it necessary to talk about this? Why is time management important in relationships? The twenty-four hours of a day is hardly enough time in a day anymore, this has affected a lot of families terribly. Some work ten hours a day and spend the remaining time in traffic. When you get home, you may have, more work to do, house chores to attend and maybe even kids to take care of.

There is pressure from work, pressure at home, too little time, you are tired, your partner is exhausted, and you both must make things work. You would think with technology, life would be easier, yet there is hardly enough time for all these things. How do we make things work despite the shortness deficit?

CONSIDER YOUR INDIVIDUAL SELF

We are naturally selfish. It takes a lot of discipline not to partner with a selfish nature. A little at a time, individuals may come to let go of this innate selfish nature, but at times, it rears up its head again. Sometimes however, this selfish nature is instinctive, and it helps us prevent a situation where we burnout.

Often people think that the solution to every problem in a relationship is to spend more time together. This approach can sometimes do more harm than good to a relationship. Can you genuinely desire what you never miss? Spend too much time together, and contempt can block out any appreciation for your partner. I think of it as self-induced cabin fever. Making some time for your self allows you to practice self-care. A moment to pursue your passions while having a little vacation away from your responsibilities as a partner and parent does a world of good.

If there is too much togetherness as a couple, desire can dwindle as resentment grows. It becomes too easy to lose appreciation than if you're never apart. Too much time together as a couple can also make it difficult to manage your moods. The emotional atmosphere can be hijacked by one person's sour mood, leaving the other partner to ride out the storm. But when you spend some time alone, you rejoin your relationship roles with energy and possibly new insights into your appreciation for your loved ones.

A little bit of space in a relationship allows longing and works to reignite passion's flame. All sorts of wonderful things can happen if you take a little time to nurture yourself. Just be sure that you don't fall into the trap of spending too much time in this role. Resentments can easily develop when one partner feels they are too alone in a relationship. After spending time alone, make sure to take time to devote to your other roles.

THINK - WE, US, YOU AND ME

Many folks look back at the beginning of their relationship with fondness. You remember all the dates, trips, and happy times you spent discovering each other. Then work, PTA meetings, the lawn, all these things suddenly conspired to take over your life. Your relationship is left longing.

There are three main ways to make time for your partnership. First, you have to make time to talk, go on a date, and connect physically. This time to talk includes conversations about what is working well and what serves as challenges in your relationship. During this time, discuss everything that needs to be discussed for your relationship to move ahead. Making time to communicate about your relationship will help you prevent future conflicts and further strengthen your partnership. It is a time of working together against the chaos of the world.

Taking time to have a date night is also very important. Life cannot be all work, a night to focus on connecting and enjoyment goes a long way in strengthening a relationship. This night out could be anything from a fancy dinner, to a walk around a town lake. Just taking a little time to reestablish your romantic connection will secure your relationship. These moments together, deposits into your relationship's emotional bank account so that when you need to make a withdrawal in the future, your relationship can withstand it. In other words, if you're connecting as a couple, then it's easier to ask for some individual time later.

Make our time for your erotic needs. As couples grow older, this piece of the marriage is too often sacrificed. Many couples find it difficult to maintain an erotic life. How can you do this in this hectic world?

Spend time together after the kids are in bed. We know the tactics children use to delay "lights out" by crying because they don't want to go to bed. Set a bedtime for your children each day. We believe children aged 1-8 should not be up past 9 pm each night. It's tempting to give in to prevent bedtime struggles, but you and your spouse need time together just as much as your kids need sleep. Set a bedtime for your children and stick to it.

One quick question before we continue. Why do a lot of couples have their kids in their bed? Why spend so much acquiring another bedroom if they were meant to sleep in your room anyway. We suggest that your bedroom is not your kids' bedroom; let them sleep in their own room! It is the sanctuary (bedroom) for you and your spouse. If you want to keep your intimate time with your spouse (which is essential), keep your kids out of your bed! Your spouse is your main priority, always remember that.

You also have to make time to connect with your partner physically. Now, we are not saying that you jot down in your planner a time to be intimate with your partner. That would be absurd. All we are saying is set up a time to physically connect with your partner and honor it, do what feels right at that moment. It could be a massage, a shower together or sex. It isn't about the activity that you do; it's about maintaining your physical connection to help maintain your relationship.

FAMILY

The last thing that requires time management is your family; be it your children, extended family, or family of choice. Everybody within the extended family and the nuclear family always want a piece of your time. You have to call your mother or father, wish a sister happy birthday, attend one occasion or the other, take care of the children, and pick up your spouse when you would have preferred to simply take a nice nap.

Obligations tend to reign in this area of our lives. Many people find it challenging to set time boundaries with family. How do we manage to make time as individual, or for our partners? Yes, talking to mom is important, but is it so important that you interrupt sexual intimacies to talk to mom when there is no real emergency? Using your time wisely in marriage requires that you know where to draw the line. It is tricky to manage time for yourself, your relationship, and your family as there will always be a need for more. But setting boundaries with time and maintaining them will most certainly help your love last.

CHAPTER FIVE

LACK OF APPRECIATION

Gratitude is "the quality of being thankful; readiness to show appreciation for and to return kindness." As children, we're taught to say "thank you" automatically in return for a favor. On this surface level, we are taught that gratitude is an appropriate social response. At the same time, on a more complex level, gratitude is a spiritual way of being. When we genuinely feel gratitude, we experience deep awe and appreciation for the goodness of something outside ourselves. Having gratitude toward someone or something means respecting its value and treasuring how unique, beautiful or indispensable it is.

Gratitude is an integral part of healthy relationships. As marriages move past the honeymoon stage, couples go from appreciating and loving every little detail about each other to taking each other for granted. We see this as a cause of trouble in many relationships. You get used to having [your spouse] in your life so much, that you forget why you chose to be with them. At this point, you become deadened to your spouse's special qualities and instead focus on things that annoy you about the person. These doldrums leave couples confused and discouraged. "Maybe the man they married isn't great after all," they say. "What happened to the spark in our relationship? What do we do *now*?"

A study was carried out on fifty committed couples, the couples were given a week to fill out appreciation journals. On days when one partner reported feeling more appreciated, he or she tended to appreciate his or her partner more the next day. Couples who had ongoing reciprocal appreciation were less likely to break up in the next nine months and they were even reported to being more committed at the end of that time. What then does this prove?

Gratitude and appreciation is necessary for maintaining long and healthy relationships.

A nourishing cycle of encouragement and appreciation provides extra incentive to maintain our relationships. In other words, when we appreciate our partners, we develop trust and respect. When we feel appreciated, we feel needed and encouraged.

SHOWING APPRECIATION

Your affection is of no consequence, if you cannot show it. How else would your spouse know that you appreciate them, if you do not make your feelings known either by voicing your appreciation vocally or showing your appreciation using body language?

The key to sparking healthy relationships with gratitude is to take the initiative. Instead of just waiting for the other person to make you feel good, jumpstart that cycle and take it into your own hands by focusing on what's good in your relationship. Start with small and achievable goals, such as giving your spouse five compliments a day, or smiling at her more often.

Touch each other as often as possible, as a means of showing appreciation. A little physical encouragement such as handholding or a pat on the leg maybe all the encouragement your spouse needs, and it can go a long way to make your marriage turn around and work out for good.

Tell your partner simple and sweet words that would make them happy. It does not cost as much to do so, at least it does not consume as much time and resources as it takes to file for a divorce. What's the worst that could happen! To this end, it is okay to say things like "I am glad you came into my life, you balance me well." Or "what would I do without you?" By so doing, we tell the other person we still care as we show appreciation.

There is one other way of showing your spouse that you appreciate them, it is by listening to them. When your partner is talking, lean in, make eye contact, and respond thoughtfully to what they are saying. Make it clear that you listening to them and digesting what they are saying. In this way, you will be showing that you value your spouse's opinion.

Gratitude is a skill that you cultivate—nurture it in yourself, and soon you will see positivity radiate back at you. What you sow is what you will reap. If you feel that the other person does not appreciate you enough, then, start out appreciating him or her, and pretty soon you will get it back.

There exists three A's in any healthy relationship, and *Appreciation* happens to be one of them. The remaining two are *Acceptance* and *Acknowledgment*. As a keen observer, a common thing I happen to notice among many couples is appreciation, or, to be more precise, the lack thereof. And this appears to be an increasingly common problem with couples who have been together for a while. This is not supposed to be so.

JUST HOW IMPORTANT IS APPRECIATION IN A HEALTHY RELATIONSHIP?

I feel, we always crave for positive attention. And appreciating someone is the best way to go about doing it. The problem starts when we don't notice or simply do not recall how we slipped into the habit of taking each other for granted. This leads to other problems like arguments, frustration, and resentment. Then, we begin to wonder if the relationship is meant to work out and before long, everything goes haywire.

Let's look at a simple, and probably not too uncommon, scenario. Your partner always drops your kid(s) off to school. He, or she, has been doing it for a while now. But you never told them how much you appreciate them for it or acknowledged how thankful you are for it. What if your partner stopped one day? You would have to adjust your schedule for it, probably start getting up slightly early in the morning, or stop watching your favorite breakfast show as you prepare to leave for work every day. What appears to be a simple thing suddenly becomes important when it doesn't get done!

Develop a habit of thanking and appreciating your spouse for things they do. Don't think that there is no need to thank someone for a something they were supposed to do anyway. You are both in a partnership, as equals. You are both working together to make the partnership work, but where one person is made to feel like they are irrelevant in a partnership, they may decide to leave. Appreciation is a key to any relationship. Appreciating someone makes them feel good about what they do. It makes them feel better about themselves, urging them to go on with new vigor. Adopt this attitude, and you will see your marriage get better from here on.

HOW DO YOU KNOW IF YOUR PARTNER DOESN'T FEEL APPRECIATED?

Some signs may suggest that you may have been taking things for granted in your relationship and your partner feels unappreciated because of that:

- When your partner gets into arguments over trivial things, watch it.
- When your spouse starts acting more emotional.
- If your spouse becomes quieter than usual, check yourself.
- If they don't ask for your opinion any more.
- If they make plans without even consulting you, be careful, you are headed for a dangerous zone.
- When they are not enthusiastic about special occasions anymore.
- They don't try to be romantic anymore.
- They appear more distant.
- Or when they begin to have an affair.

HOW DO YOU SHOW YOUR APPRECIATION TO YOUR PARTNER?

Here are some things that you may want to try:

- Pay full attention when your partner speaks with you, making full eye contact. This assures them that you appreciate whatever it is that they have to tell you.
- Thanking them for unimportant things makes a significant difference. Appreciate them if they iron your clothes or cook your food.
- Appreciate anything that adds value to your relationship, and tell your partner what you appreciate, regularly.
- Let your partner know that you don't take them for granted just because they have been doing something every day for the last year. "I really appreciate you doing the dishes every night after supper." Or, "Darling, I love how you keep my things ready as I prepare to dress for work. It feels so special."
- Appreciate them for being there with you through your difficulties. They are the ones investing their time in you more than anyone else!

- Acknowledge what you love about your partner, their family, and their friends.
- Compliment them on simple things – "I love how that yellow dress of yours makes you look radiant."
- Enjoy your time together, be playful, laugh and have fun while appreciating each other.
- Most importantly, appreciate and express your love for your partner regularly. Healthy relationships are the ones that keep evolving and when it comes to love, appreciating someone is never enough.

When you have invested so much into a relationship, it feels lovely to get a pat on the back for the efforts. Make appreciating your partner a priority to keep the spark alive.

CHAPTER SIX

MONEY TROUBLE

*M*oney is an invaluable commodity. It can be used in a multitude of ways to increase personal welfare, satisfaction, pleasure, excitement, joy, contentment, and so on. It can be used as a means of exchange in return for goods and services, or given out as a gift, or used for an investment, or piled up in the bank. It is one property that surpasses the rest, and simply knowing that you have it gives you a feeling of security. Once you have enough of it, you no longer need to be preoccupied with how much something costs. You can simply buy whatever one most desires and derive the maximum gratification from it. Money is a beautiful thing to have, until it begins to mess with your marriage and happiness.

We've known marriages that have survived infidelity several times over, but money, money is a HUGE issue. Some have said, 'Discuss money or it will discuss you.' This is true. When spending and saving habits are not the same, disagreements occur, which then turns into loud arguments and then into fights and deep resentment. Money is a *big* marriage dissolver.

No question about it. Fighting over money is hazardous to your relationship. One recent study found that the more frequently couples argued over finances, the more likely they were to get divorced, especially if their altercations occurred several times a week, or almost every day.

Couples fight about many things, it is normal to have altercations, whether in the form of a disagreement over child-rearing methods, sex, household chores, relations with in-laws or any other problem. But, where money is concerned, it could be the root cause of divorce.

Financial management has become an area of contention, where attitudes of prideful self-righteousness are most likely to prevail. When couples argue about money, their respective positions profoundly reflect core values that it's hard for them *not* to get into antagonistic gridlock on the subject. And like a festering disease, as time passes such polarization tends not to get better but worse, ultimately threatening the very foundation of their relationship.

The inability of most couples to appreciate and sympathetically discuss their conflicting attitudes toward money eventuates in all kinds of misunderstandings and feeling of hurt, which in turn results in an increasing sense of alienation and loss of affection.

Although typically many variations are in play, there are two essential positions that people take toward money. And, regrettably, these differing viewpoints or perspectives aren't reconcilable. This is the reason why it is crucial that couples learn how to amicably agree to disagree on the matter. Let both spouses sit down and come to a recognition of the other persons view point, understand each other's dissimilar view on money, find a way around these money problems and respect each other's views.

To help you understand a bit more about the differences between partners, here are the two eternally contrasting monetary philosophies, and the labels that best portray them. There are *the Spender* (seen unfavorably by their contrary partner as a "spendthrift." "squanderer," or "compulsive shopper"). They enjoy spending the money without too much thought. *The Saver* (seen unfavorably by their contrary partner as a "cheapskate," "tightwad," "hoarder," or even "miser") however are a different case altogether. They cherish money, and hold it in high esteem, preferring to save and invest than spend it unnecessarily.

The irreconcilable difference between couples' discrepant belief systems on this commodity can easily fuel relational conflict, *independent* of the couples' actual financial issues. With time, this conflict could grow worse if their funds are seriously in deficient. Knowing each partner's beliefs and monetary perceptions go a long way in helping partners organize themselves better and in the end improve their understanding of each other.

We have stressed the importance of couples' explicitly and empathically discussing their money differences if they're to alleviate abiding financial tensions between them. And to ensure that such communication is productive, we strongly suggest they both reflect upon the above spender/saver dichotomy. Even beyond this exploration, however, it's imperative that, in advance, they painstakingly evaluate all the things that, personally, money *means* to them. Professionals who've written about this complicated subject agree that fights about money aren't about this medium of exchange at all. Instead, they're about what money *signifies*. And what it represents for one person can diverge markedly from what it symbolizes for the other.

Permitting yourself to be as objective, and as truthful, with yourself as possible, consider whether and *how* your attitude toward money relates to:

- The love, care, and affection you shower on your partner.
- A sense of safety, security, and stability you feel.
- The feelings of competence, power and control.
- Your self-worth. Do you feel that you're worth spending money on, or having money spent on you?
- Do you think that the money you have results in your being acceptable?
- Your status and making a positive impression on others.
- Being materially rewarded for your efforts and achievements.
- Your overall success. Do you view your wealth as a sign that you are getting somewhere on the success ladder?
- Warranted self-indulgence.
- Gaining others' respect and maybe improving *your* self-respect as well.
- Sense of personal responsibility.
- Sexual opportunity and possibly also sexual *dominance*.
- Your freedom and independence in life.
- Developing companionship and warmth.
- A sense of contentment.
- The feeling empowerment or enrichment.
- Filling a void or deprivation in your life.
- Achieving happiness and a state of well-being.

In discussing money issues with your partner, it's critical that you keep an open mind. Remember, this isn't about winning a deadly battle, or endlessly debating whose "talking points" are superior. No, it's about recognizing that your partner's outlook on money may have just as much validity as your own. And, additionally, may be held with just as much pride, conviction, and commitment.

Consider also that the two of you may possess different inborn tendencies, temperaments, and histories. Growing up, you have both received from your caregivers, largely different *messages* about money. Viewing your marital money problems in an expanded light may help you realize that what struck you as wrong about your spouse, now makes a lot more sense, is more warranted and is legitimate. Lastly, it cannot be overemphasized that you and your mate, must be willing to adopt a positive mindset, searching for common ground and areas of mutually acceptable compromise. For both of your belief systems—and *emotions*—about money must be considered if you're to negotiate your financial conflicts and resolve them successfully.

It's hardly realistic to expect that either of you can transform your well-entrenched, firmly held values about money. But it's certainly reasonable to think that with increased knowledge, compassion, acceptance, and respect toward each other's perspective, you'll be able to put an end to what may long have been a relational thorn in *both* your sides.

CHAPTER SEVEN

RESIST TECHNOLOGICAL INTERFERENCE

We're living in an age where we have electronic tools that were only dreamed of by past generations. Things we never thought possible have become part of our everyday lives Within the past fifteen years, the technological advances available to us have skyrocketed so fast that most of us can't keep up.

Many of these new electronic tools and gadgets are supposed to make communication easier. Email, text messaging, and cell phones should make it easier to share information and communicate, so we can be in constant contact with anyone we wish. It sounds like it should improve our communication, doesn't it?

The truth is, electronics seem to be causing problems for a lot of married couples. Instead of helping communication, they seem to be a barrier. Instead of allowing for more time together, they seem to be taking away quality time together for many couples. Instead of making work more manageable, it seems to encourage many people to take their work home with them. There are just too many things going on online, the real world doesn't seem so real anymore. Some people practically live online or on air. Your banks are online, you can watch movies online, you can watch the news online, you can order things from mobile stores, you can order your food and any other thing you need online. Life feels much easier online or on television, than it feels in the real world. Maybe that is why a lot of people just want to transition out of this reality into the virtual world. But can your marriage survive online?

Having access to the latest technology isn't a bad thing and doesn't have to be bad for your marriage. You can have a meaningful marriage and still interact with technology in the real world. You just have to learn to set some limits and monitor your usage.

Taking some proactive steps to address your use of electronics can be very helpful to your relationship. The time spent unduly on the internet or in front of the television could be spent on with your spouse, you and that one person alone.

BE THERE; GIVE YOUR SPOUSE YOUR ATTENTION.

When your spouse tries to say something to you while you are watching television, are you guilty of not paying attention? If you are using the computer do you sometimes respond with "yep" or "uh huh" but have no idea what your spouse just said to you? Do you send text messages while riding in the car together, during dinner, or while you are on a date together? These are just a few examples of ways in which technology can interfere with a couple's quality times. Relationships are harder now because conversation becomes texting, arguments take place over a phone call and feelings become a status updates.

It is essential to set aside technology each day and make time for each other. And when you are spending time together, make sure you can be present with your spouse and not checking your email or answering text messages.

SET LIMITS ON ELECTRONICS USAGE

Talk to your spouse about what time frame seems like a reasonable amount of time to use electronics each day. Perhaps two hours of television and computer time seems like a reasonable limit. Or maybe you think 30 minutes a day is enough. Each couple will have a different limit depending on your schedules and responsibilities.

Then, without making any changes, spend one week, keeping track of how much time you spend using your cell phone, using the computer, playing video games, or watching television. Write it down each day. This can be eye-opening for many people. Most people underestimate how much time they spend using electronics each day and are surprised to see how many hours they spend using electronics.

Once you are aware of how much time you spend using the electronics, develop a plan to decrease your use if necessary. Replace time you usually spend watching television with talking to your spouse. Instead of communicating via text message or social media, spend time together. Plan a date night. Get outside together. Do something together that can help build your relationship?

Agree to leave your cell phone at home when you go on dates together. If the thought of this invokes feelings of panic, remember that not too long ago, people didn't have cell phones and they survived just fine. If you can't bear not having it, turn it on silent and avoid continually checking to see if you are missing anything. The point is to give your spouse the attention.

ENGAGE IN ELECTRONICS FAST

Be willing to take a more radical approach to decreasing your dependence on electronics? Consider an "electronics fast!" Spend just one week without the television, computer, and other electronics. Can't imagine giving up everything for a whole week? Try this approach with just one thing, such as television.

Giving up electronics for a short period will help you reconnect. It can remind you of how to spend quality time together doing something that doesn't involve technology. It can help you rediscover other things you like to do and can make a big difference in your relationship.

Even if you don't "fast" from electronics, consider setting some ground rules. For example, turn off the television during dinner. Shut off the computer an hour before you go to bed. These rules can help ensure that you are interacting with each other.

DO YOU NEED TO KNOW EACH OTHER'S INTERNET PASSWORDS?

Login credentials have become a significant part of our everyday lives. They keep our information safe (supposedly) and allow us access to our accounts from almost anywhere. But in many marriages, these passwords become a barrier to intimacy.

I know that we've all gone security crazy over the past couple of decades, and it's entirely possible you think I'm nuts to suggest married couples share their information. But *security* and *privacy* are two different things. If a person tells me that they aren't sharing their internet accounts with their spouse because they have reason to believe their spouse will harm them in some way- that makes sense. You need feel safe.

But when a person tells me that they aren't giving their spouse access to their Facebook account because they deserve their *privacy*, I'm calling a flag on the play. What privacy? I don't remember that being part of the marriage deal. When I get up in the morning, my wife sees me in all my unadorned, pudgy gutted, hairy-legged, bad-breath glory. If ever there were a time when she might wish that I would want privacy… that might be it. But the truth is marriage and privacy don't mix.

When you choose to spend the rest of your life together, transparency is part of the deal. When you sign those papers that confirm you both as a legally married couple, you are telling the world, that you have both gone past a point of seeking seclusion from each other, and that this is the one person you want to show everything to. If this is the case, why would you then want to hide the password to your phone or Facebook account from them?

My wife and I made a decision a long time ago to share our account information and passwords for email and social media accounts. There are no corners of the internet to which only I have the key. As far as I know, my wife might be accessing my Facebook right now. If she is, good for her.

I want her to feel that she can see what's going on in my life. She can read my emails if she'd like. She can view my internet history if she wants. An invasion of my privacy? I don't think so. It's an invitation to intimacy. An invitation to know all of me.

Besides, there's another added benefit to this. By giving Angela access to my internet activity, I have increased my accountability in this area. It reminds me not to make online decisions I wouldn't want my wife to see. That's a strong incentive to do the right thing.

Oh, I know that we've all grown up hearing that "character is what you do when no one else is watching" but, character is also our willingness to invite others to examine our actions. Chaperones may be out of style in the current dating culture, but you have to admit, their presence did have a way of keeping things "G" rated.

I know that sharing account information isn't always possible. Your work may have strict guidelines for your login credentials and email accounts. I'm certainly not suggesting you break those rules. All I am saying is that you bare yourself to your partner as much as you can, and do not draw lines that would serve to breach the intimacy.

And if you're in a relationship with an abuser who would use your personal information against you or harm you in some way, I'm also not suggesting you give them the keys to your online presence. I'm talking to people like me, people who have recreational accounts- personal email, Facebook, twitter, you-tube. People who have no *good* reason to block their spouse from having access.

If that's you, I'm just making the humble suggestion that giving your spouse access to your online life may be one of the greatest ways you can build trust in your relationship.

CHAPTER EIGHT

NON-NEGOTIABLES OF LOVE

Love is patient, love is kind and is not jealous; love does not brag and is not arrogant it does not act unbecomingly; it does not seek its own, is not provoked, does not take into account a wrong suffered, does not rejoice in unrighteousness, but rejoices with the truth; bears all things, believes all things, hopes all things, endures all things. Love never fails. (1Corinthians13:4-8a)

Non-negotiable are those things you will not negotiate. They follow your values and principles and define not only what you will and won't accept from others, but also what you will and won't accept from yourself. They are the big-time deal breakers. They are the promises you keep to yourself, your family and your team. That is what love is, it is non-negotiable.

Love is a must have in your marriage. You cannot afford to give up love in a relationship. Regardless of scope, love is non-negotiable because you do not sacrifice your love; you give it wholly, no matter what. Once you have committed to love someone for the rest of your lives, you have got to love that someone, without a second thought on that horrible personality or behavior they display. Everybody has a flaw. Loving your spouse in marriage requires loving that person wholeheartedly.

Categorizing your love as non-negotiable is critical for a successful, long-term relationship. The love non-negotiable areas of any relationship are areas of concern that allow us to show and receive love, ensuring we are satisfied in a relationship. The question then is how do you define these, how do you share them, and what role should they play in your relationship?

If you are in a relationship and haven't already had this type of conversation, please be encouraged to talk with your partner about your love for them and get them to come to an understanding of the fact that you will stand by them no matter what. Tell your partner that you are going to love them regardless if they love you. Tell them your core values are important and you are committed to those beliefs. Those core values will guide you and your love life principles. That is why they are called non-negotiable.

If you decide to take your love life seriously and establish your love non-negotiable, your love life will change, and you will see transformations in your partner and in your relationship as you grow together. You are different people now as compared to when you first met, and you can enjoy each other just as much if not more. Your relationship can grow even richer.

Loving relentlessly can be a tough thing to do. Things get in the way: emotions, patience, self-esteem, and the will-to-fight. This happens because most people don't learn how to keep their love on full blast in the face of pain and fear. Sometimes it's the hardest thing to do. But if you want to build healthy relationships with God and others, learning to keep your love on is non–negotiable.

Adults and children alike thrive in healthy relationships where it is safe to love and be loved, to know and be known. Yet for many, relationships are anything but safe, loving, or intimate. Anxiety, manipulation, control, and conflict define them. The reason is that most people have never been trained to be powerful enough to keep their love on in the face of mistakes, pain, and fear. Love is non-negotiable, it leaves you with the power to draw healthy boundaries, communicate in love, and ultimately protect your connections so you can love against all the odds. As a result, your relationships will be radically transformed for eternity.

Your love for your spouse ought to be non-negotiable, it is not a seasonal thing. It is an all-weather love. A non-negotiable love is a love that moves past all obstacles, a love that is meek enough to forgive, and a love that is careful enough to accept and forsake.

Part of the vows we make at the altar is to love our spouse and share our lives with them. This love is not to be shown only when a partner is faithful, it extends to even those times when the partner slips up and falls into adultery. Love is forgiveness, letting go, and leaning in again. True love as we've seen, bears all things and forgives. True love is non-negotiable love.

This true love was exemplified in the Bible, Christ came to suffer and die for us, while we were yet sinners. He took us as dirty as we were and washed us clean. He holds us and helps us through the stages of unbelief, through times when we fall into sin, till we grow into adult Christians and even then, he is ever willing to move past our transgressions and still love us. What other example vividly expresses the fact that the love you ought to have for your spouse is the kind of non-negotiable love that Christ has already shown.

CHAPTER NINE

THE AGE LONG ISSUE OF FORGIVENESS

Lack of forgiveness or unwillingness to forgive has wrecked a great many homes. Forgiving your spouse can be very hard to do, especially if the offenses feel personal, but you must not make excuses and put off doing it any longer. Forgiving is the most important lesson you are here (in the classroom of life) to learn, and the consequences of putting it off are a great deal of pain and suffering for YOU and your family.

I'm sorry, but I'm going to be blunt here, "I'm not ready" is an excuse you use when you can't articulate the real reason you don't *want* to forgive. You need to identify the real reason you don't want to forgive so you can work past it.

Do you think staying angry toward your spouse protects you from further mistreatment and that forgiving would allow more of it? Is staying mad (and casting them as the bad guy) allowing you to avoid looking at your own faults, mistakes or pain? I have had many spouses admit that if they released their anger toward their spouse they would have to deal with their faults and that is just too painful.

Are you using anger and hurt as an excuse to keep your spouse away from you, because you have issues with intimacy (discomfort or lack of desire) and you would rather avoid it? Is your anger justifying or giving you a reason not to have a healthy intimate relationship?

Do you feel like your spouse hasn't been punished enough? The truth is, it's healthy for people to understand the wrong and then let it go and move forward without guilt. Drawing out the shame and guilt isn't necessary for someone to change. Are you always trying to be right? Have you cast your spouse as the bad one in the marriage in order to feel good about yourself? Be honest.

Here is the truth:

- Staying mad doesn't protect you from further mistreatment. Proper boundaries enforced with strength and love do. You can forgive and still be safe. Remember always that the Bible says that love conquers all things. If you employ love instead of anger, would that not be more effective in changing the situation?
- You are here on this planet to work on fixing YOU. That should and must be your focus. You must stop pointing fingers and work on growing, learning and becoming more loving yourself. That is your job.
- If you have issues with intimacy, you must stop avoiding them and get help so that YOU can have a happy, prosperous, and fulfilling life. Staying mad at your spouse and avoiding intimacy will never create happiness.
- Forgiving does not require the other person to be punished or repent first. If you wait for that, you will only be hurting yourself and your family.
- Every day you have to choose if you would rather be right or happy. Your ego wants to be right, but it's the wrong choice.
- You have every right to be hurt, but you don't have the right to be hurtful.

Here are a couple of principles of truth that will help you to forgive now:

Remember you aren't perfect either. Get off your high horse. Your spouse did wrong, and it sounds like this was an especially painful thing, but you aren't perfect either. You may not have made this mistake, but you have made other mistakes, and I guarantee there is a downside to being married to you too (there is for all of us).

You must remember that you are both imperfect, struggling students in the classroom of life, with a lot more to learn. You both deserve forgiveness. You alone are responsible for the pain you are experiencing. No situation can cause you pain without your participation in it because your thoughts and feelings are in your control. No one can take away your pain, you are in charge of your life solely. You alone have that power.

If you come to understand this principle, once you grasp the truth that you are in control of your thoughts and feelings, you don't have to wait until you feel ready to forgive. You can choose to be ready. Your spouse may be guilty of bad choices, but they are not less of a person than you are. You both have the same infinite and absolute value. You both have the same value no matter how many mistakes you both make.

This is true because life is a classroom, not a test, and your value isn't on the line. That does not mean you and your spouse don't have more to learn or a need to improve your behavior. Your lack of knowledge and need for improvement does not affect your value.

Forgiveness is about seeing yourself and others accurately — as innocent, wholly forgiven, struggling, scared, messed up, but perfect students in the classroom of life. Most of us think forgiving is about seeing people as guilty and then trying to pardon them for those mistakes. If you try to forgive this way, it will never happen. You will still be hung up on the fact they are guilty.

Forgiveness will never work when it's a gift undeserved. Real forgiveness means letting go of judgment entirely and understanding that God has already forgiven all the wrongs, pain and hurt on both sides of this. The entire past has been wiped clean of all selfish, fear-based behavior. It is gone except for the resentment you are holding onto. It is time to let go and accept forgiveness for both of you.

You must give each other permission to be a "work in progress" and not crucify the next person for mistakes. Forgiveness is the key to happiness. It is the only way to peace, confidence, and security. This is just universal law. The key to forgiveness lies in one straightforward choice that you must make over and over every day. You must take every day as a new day and let go of all the hurts from yesterday.

That you forgive however does not mean that your consciousness totally blots out the event from your memory. But when those memories filter in, deliberately choose not to hold them against your spouse in this new day. Trust again, love again, strive for happiness and for your own peace, and the peace of those around you.

What energy do you want to live in: Judgment energy or forgiveness energy?

The energy you generate and accumulate around you, determines the response you give out. If you pick the negative energy, and turn to judgment and lack of forgiveness, you will only push your spouse away and cause more troubles for the both of you. But if you create and surround yourself with positive energy, your marriage can thrive on forgiveness, and you can both spend your time together for a long time.

This judgment energy means you stand in judgment of others, condemning and crucifying them for past mistakes. If you choose this, you must understand that it will also create low self-esteem in you. This happens because you are giving power to the idea that people are "not good enough" and this will subconsciously spill over upon you as well. This judgment mindset does not permit forgiveness, and it always harbors anger and resentment. Adopting this mindset, means adopting stress and heart aches. This is not a good and gratifying way to live.

When you have a forgiveness mindset, you choose to forgive yourself and others and completely let go of every misconceived, selfish, and fear-based mistake either of you has ever made. You choose to see these mistakes for what they are — bad choices born of confusion, self-doubt, lack of knowledge, low self-esteem and fear. In this place of forgiveness, choose to see everyone as innocent and forgiven (by God) for all mistakes and in doing so, you start over on a clean slate every day. If you choose this mindset, you will feel safe, loved, whole and good about yourself all the time as the energy that comes with this state is light, peaceful and happy.

CHAPTER TEN

THE FOUR SEASONS OF MARRIAGE

Just as there is a time and season for everything, there are times and seasons in marriage. As couples grow together, their age could lead to separation, or it could work to help strengthen their love. The four stages of marital relations are:

THE HONEYMOON SEASON

This is the first stage after marriage. The honeymoon stage is a period when love and passionate attraction binds a couple together and leads to commitment. The passion stage is very strong and significant. It is a wave of feel-good brain chemicals orchestrated by nature to make the two of you forsake all others and take action to ensure the survival of the species.

Even if you marry later in life, or for the second time, nature supplies these delicious bursts of neurotransmitters to make you bond. Couples not only frolic and fall madly in love during the passion stage, but they begin to establish the trust, respect and emotional intimacy that will support their relationship forever

This stage however is as transient as springtime. After two or more years pass by, most couples begin to lose that initial magic, and the sparks dwindle. Too many people are familiar with the first stage, couples fondly remember this special time of falling in love with each other and the intense feelings that rippled through them during that time and most wonder- what happened to that spark?

Those are times when life was so wonderful, you could not stand to live without the other person. Your thoughts often turned to the other when you were not with them. You fell in love and knew that this was the person you wanted to be with the rest of our life. Little differences between you seemed cute and endearing, and all that mattered was being together. No matter how much you saw other couples going through struggles, you knew that was not you. They did not have what you had as a couple. You had your plans mapped out, life was going to be wonderful, and everything would be perfect. In your minds, you knew these intense feelings of love would last forever, but alas! That was not to be.

THE SEASON OF DISENCHANTMENT

I really don't think I like you as much as I thought.

At some point, those little differences that at first were endearing in our spouse, start to annoy us. We begin to feel bothered by the way our spouse is different and does not always agree with our plans and ideas. The self-talk in the back of our mind starts wondering why our spouse cannot be more like us.

Little unpleasant habits we often ignored in the past, becomes a big deal. Why does she bite her nails, why does it smell so bad after he uses the toilet, why does he always drop his dirty shirt on the floor and never pick them up afterwards? You find out that you get irritated easily about your partner's behavior and things don't seem as rosy and lovey-dovey as they first were. Signs such as these mark the entry into the second stage of marriage, *the disenchant stage*, as we realize at this stage that our spouse has values, goals and ideals that may not align with our own. And this is where marriage really begins.

During the disenchant stage, we start to realize that our spouse is not the perfect person that we had envisioned him or her to be. Sometimes, especially if our romance stage had been particularly intense, we are hurt deeply by this disenchantment, but this is where love is strained and tested.

We realize that the expectations we had of the perfect marriage is not playing out as we expected. For some, this realization is too heart wrenching that the marriage may not survive it. it is the stage where too many give up on the marriage and get divorced. During this stage of disenchant, you gradually desire to be away from each other because you are no longer blindly in love. Your eyes have become open to some or all of your partner's flaws. While some opt for divorce at this stage because it is easier, other couples simply accept this as the status quo and allow these frustrations to continue to build up over time.

When you find yourself in this stage, you don't just choose to remain as housemates, trying to live it out, following the usual routine. The best approach is not to file for a divorce either. Stick with each other and try to work through their problems during this disenchantment stage. Seek the counsel of family, friends, clergy and marriage or family counselors. You can find the key to unlocking the stores of marital bliss if you relate with people who have been through that stage.

Many people continue to struggle in marriage, while their troubles worsen. Marriage trouble may worsen quickly, but most often, it occurs gradually, over time. It can begin with a gradual growing apart or constant disagreement and fighting. Then later, the marriage may ride down a dark path due to drug, alcohol or other addictions. Sometimes infidelity, such as an online relationship, pornography addiction, or an outright affair can also cause severe anguish and grief that would serve to further separate the couples.

As the couple finds themselves in this second stage of marriage, they must know that they are on their way to the third stage; that is misery stage, which is a stage marked by a widening separation, distance, frustration, anger and an obvious absence of closeness, acceptance, and love.

THE MISERY SEASON

The misery stage is a stage where many couples find themselves considering a marriage separation or divorce. Many believe the pain is too intense at this stage. This stage is like gang wars, both parties go after each for very trivial reasons. This stage breeds a lot of intent! It just may seem that too much has happened and there is no way to forgive and love and move on. Many judge that the restoration of love and trust seems impossible and it may seem that things can never be the same.

When children are involved, this third stage of misery is particularly difficult on them. Regardless of whether the couple stays together in misery or divorce, the misery of the marriage relationship often begins to affect the children negatively. Most families are in this stage. The pain is often so intense during the misery stage that it is common to only want it to *STOP*.

Much like the pain of a toothache that consumes your whole being, you cannot seem to think of anything else besides stopping the pain. One spouse may be pushing hard for the divorce, while the other wants to stop divorce and is resistant. Love is tested, often to the absolute limit during this time of trial. If the couple ends the marriage at this point and remarry other partners, they are significantly more likely to repeat the same mistakes and experience the effects of yet another divorce with their second or third spouse. The best way to handle this period in marriage is to try and work it out.

THE WINNING SEASON

This is the stage of marriage, where the scores count. You have played the game, you have fought and struggled for the ball, you have had your moments of frustration and anger, but have you triumphed, have you scored? You would not have scored if you opt out of your marriage because it has become too hard. You would not have scored if you run away from your marriage because the sweet part is no more. You would not have won, if you did not go through the hard process to come out victorious.

Most people whose marriages end in divorce are not bad people. Rather, they are just people who were not patient enough to work it out. They are often people who never learned the proper tools for a happy marriage. They just found someone, fell in love and thought well the marriage would last on love alone.

Marriage does not last on love alone. *Coaching Married Couples by a Couple Coaching* helps to point you in the right direction when it comes to marriage. Coaching helps you figure out what you ought to do together. You can find the way forward in your marriage together, instead of letting the marriage crash.

We both have experienced all four stages of marriage, and we survived and came out stronger. Instead of giving up, we found solutions, we won. We gathered experiences and learned from them. We learned that certain tools are needed to improve marriage and when they are in place, couples live in a happy and harmonious marriage. We learned that marriage does not follow the romance and "happily ever after" and the "white picket fence" formula portrayed in literature and media. Rather, we find that there are certain learnable skills, attitudes and tools that they can use to deal with the inevitable problems of the real world and the difficult struggles that a marriage will face each day.

You need the right skill, attitudes and tools to move your marriage from the third stage of misery into the fourth stage of winning. Learning to beat the odds of the world and staying married for a lifetime, being committed to your spouse no matter what, training yourself to have a non-negotiable love for your partner, learning to have a relationship with unconditional love, perfecting acceptance and forgiveness, and learning to make the other person feel valued is a mark of the winning stage.

The ability to be able to share yourselves, be honest with each other and be appreciated for being yourself brings a joyful feeling. Winning changes the way you live together, speak to each other, and interact with each other on a daily basis. It is a continued peace that comes from open and honest communication. It is the realization that while love is not perfect, just as we are not perfect, that it is in fact resilient and your relationship can be stronger than ever and no one can break this bond at this point no matter what come their way!

Whether you are in the disenchant stage, grieving the loss of that magical honeymoon stage, or if you have moved firmly into the misery stage, we can give you the marriage strategies you need to rebuild your marriage. While in misery, it is often hard to see that there is hope and that change is possible. But we must tell you this; *there is indeed hope*. Your marriage can be better, don't give up.

Couples have turned their marriages around by giving this program a chance.

CHAPTER ELEVEN

TEAMWORK IN MARRIAGE, MAKES THE MARRIAGE WORK

"Can two walk together, unless they are agreed?" Amos 3:3

We all watch sports, and we all love sports because we have that one team that we root for. The team maybe affiliated to us in some way, or we may just love the team, because we love the team. We often do not have elaborate reasons why we love the teams we love. We glory in their glory, we fight with the referee through our screens when we think they have not been fairly treated, we feel sad when they lose, we want them to win against the other team, just because we love them, they are our team and we don't give up on our team.

It would certainly be a surprise if a member of a team, turns against his team on the pitch and begins to play for the opposing team. He might even be booked for psychiatric evaluation by his team because his actions would not be displayed by a reasonable person. The bottom line is, we value teams, we stand with our team, despite their failures, insecurities, weaknesses and transgressions. You don't go against your team because you had some issue with them. Once you belong to a team, you celebrate your triumph together. There is nothing as exhilarating as seeing a group of individuals come together with all their differences and nuances to work together in accomplishing a common goal. They sacrifice their personal glory, for the benefit of the group and put their individuality aside so that they can work together.

After getting pumped up about a sports team achieving great things from working together, do you ever stop to think how great your marriage would be if you worked as a unified team.

Two of the most essential parts of a healthy marriage are teamwork and communication. Without those two areas being a priority, it's tough for a marriage to survive. That's fights over finances and money problems are the leading cause of divorce in America today. People often don't work as a team where money is concerned.

The popular idea about marriage is that it merges two people into one. When you both got married, you were aware of the new status you were getting into. You held a ceremony to celebrate your union and told everyone that henceforth; your life was no longer about you, it was now about you and that person. It was God's design that together, you are a team, get used to that. That is the idea that sets the tone from the time you step down the aisle and out the door as a married couple.

This means that when it comes to money, you have one bank account. You make budgets together, you stay on the same page regarding financial matters. You both need to sit down at the table and come up with a budget that you both agree on. If you do so, then surprises won't happen, and fights won't occur. Each month, before the month begins, you sit down and go over every dollar on paper on purpose.

That's why it's vital to have one primary bank account that you both use. When you have separate accounts, it's too easy to start thinking, *this is my money, and that is their money.* It is your money together. Once you have that single account, you can set a limit on a single purchase that you both make without talking. For instance, if your limit is one hundred dollars then neither of you would buy anything over one hundred dollars without talking to your spouse first. That specific number will depend on your income. It might be more, and it might be less. But it's essential that you both know what's coming in and going out of your bank account. The left-hand needs to know what the right hand is up to!

The Marriage Team

It is only a unified team that wins. What if we decide to put our selfish tendencies and individual satisfactions aside and do what the Bible says, what if we work together in accordance with God's plan and become one flesh? When couples work toward becoming one flesh, we believe that couples will represent to the world a unified team that is built to win.

As we look back, we discovered that one of the major reasons that our marriage encountered so many setbacks in the early seasons was a result of our failure to work as a team. I had to have it my way. She had to have things her way. We ended up butting heads and creating a dysfunctional team. We spent most of our time battling one another instead of working together. But we soon discovered quickly that a disjointed marriage could not function the way God designed it to function.

A Unified Marriage

It is impossible to become a unified team when you have two different visions. The futile attempt at unity can only result in division. When you have division, the vision for your marriage will die. We have overcome some intense challenges as a couple, and we are working through some even now, but we understand that the only way our marriage will become all God designed it to be is to work together.

Challenges will come and they will attack your marriage at every angle, but you must be determined to stay in the fight. You must never give up; you must never stop fighting, until you win. One can win against a thousand, but two can deal with ten thousand if they work together with one mind and in unity.

We have learned a lot in our quest for a unified team, and we desire to share the wealth of knowledge we have amassed with you. We realized seven key strategies that will fortify and elevate your marriage when you work as a team.

Here are the keys you need to make a great team:

1. Know the vision for marriage; know "your plays" and the focal point. Why did you two decide the get married, why did it seem important in the first place? Ask yourselves the questions that matter and decide what your vision is for your marriage. When you discuss and agree with your spouse on the vision you have for your marriage, begin to put your marriage vision into action. With this vision in place, you will have something to work toward and you will not have to start off aimlessly. By doing this you are working together as a team.
2. Sacrifice individual accomplishment for team victory: if you want this team to succeed, you have got to put aside your personal desires and goals to work toward the good of the team. This doesn't mean that

you should not put in effort to be better at your job, or to attain your goals in life, but as you put your team first things will work smoothly.

3. Understand your role and responsibilities in marriage: yes, you have a role. Live up to the expectations and responsibilities of your marriage. These responsibilities need not be spelled out but rather implied in most cases. Don't be that person who pulls away from responsibilities.

4. Set specific goals to achieve together. You have your whole life before you, make plans on how to live that life together. A wise man, before building a house, makes all the necessary plans. Plan out your lives together and work toward achieving those plans.

5. Know the strengths/weaknesses of your spouse. We are not all perfect, we are only mortal humans, striving for perfection. The other person may have a lot of flaws but don't hold that against them. Rather learn how to look past them or partner to help each other overcome those things together. This is one way the partnership can work.

6. Invest in your spouse: invest your time, money, affection, emotion in your spouse. Where your treasure is, there your heart will be. You most often never value things you have not worked to get, so also, a lot of people do not value their spouse, because they have not put in much effort into their union.

7. If you invest in your spouse, you will not be in a hurry to rush out of the marriage, because you have some interest to protect.

8. Finally, know your goals in marriage. Marriage is not a bed of roses or a playground for children. Marriage is serious adult stuff. Know your goals in marriage. Set goals, and work to achieve them. Don't play with your marriage, it is an expensive partnership. Treat the partnership with respect if you want it to thrive.

Your goal may be to help each other grow spiritually while loving each other. It may also be to balance each other out, or to help each other fulfill God's purpose for your lives. Whether your goal is to motivate or strengthen each other so that you both can work toward that goal and make your marriage a fruitful partnership.

FINALLY

God's love for married couples is settled in his heart. The first thing he did after creation was to unite the man and the woman. It is for the purpose of this unity that he stripped them of every external influences and this is why the man must leave his mother and father and cleave to his wife.

God realized that marriage is a lovely thing, and to those who can handle it, it is meant to strengthen them and aid them in achieving their life's purpose. This is the first purpose of marriage, to bind and strengthen. That is the purpose of a cord, to bind and strengthen, to hold together. Once you tie the knot of marriage, it brings more benefits than detriments to your doorsteps.

Our maker loves marriages, because they produce families. When a marriage is sound, the family is sound. Don't be the hand that tears apart the blessing of marriage, treat your spouse with the respect and love they deserve and focus on making your marriage better.

For those planning a trip along the road of marriage, gather as much knowledge as you can about this journey you are taking. This is the reason why most marriages fail, couples do not know where they are heading and therefore, they do not have a plan.

You are probably planning for your honeymoon as you plan your wedding. You book a hotel room, check out the nice places you could visit during that period, and you make elaborate plans for both the wedding and honeymoon. But do you ever stop to make plans for your marriage?

When organizing your wedding ceremony, never forget to make plans for the marriage that follows afterwards. That marriage goes beyond the flamboyant ceremony, so you had better be prepared for it. Our prayer is that this book prepares you for that journey ahead.

BOOKING INFORMATION

We would love to partner with you for your upcoming event, conference, marriage training or marriage coaching. We look forward partnering together to impact marriages around the world!

E-mail carletonbooker@gmail.com

Office (925) 595-8724

TheWorshipCenterChurch.org

Made in the USA
Middletown, DE
12 August 2022

70937429R00035